THE CHILDREN OF THE RIVER

NORTHWATER

CONSTANTINE ISSIGHOS

Copyright 2012 © Constantine Issighos. Published in Canada. Printed in U.S.A. No part of this book may be reproduced or transmitted in any form or by any means, electronic or mechanical, including photocopying, recording, and/or by any information storage and retrieval system except by a reviewer who may quote brief passages in a review to be printed in a magazine, newspaper, or on the web without written permission in writing from the author/publisher. For information, please contact www.awaqkunabooks.com

NorthWater is an imprint of Awaqkuna Books Inc.

Vol. 3 of THE AMAZON EXPLORATION SERIES:
THE CHILDREN OF THE RIVER

Library and Archives Canada

ISBN 978-0-9878599-2-1

Library and Archives Canada Cataloguing in Publication

ATTENTION CHILDRENS ASSOCIATIONS, BOOK STORES, PUBLIC OR PRIVATE LIBRARIES: quantity discounts are available on bulk purchases of this book series.

THE AMAZON EXPLORATION SERIES

Children's Books

by

Constantine Issighos

1	Upper Amazon Voyage by River Boat
2	The People of the River
3	The Children of the River
4	Amazon's Nature of Things
5	Echoes of Nature: a Beautiful Wild Habitat
6	The Amazon Rainforest
7	Amazonian Sisterhood
8	Amazon River Wolves
9	Amazonian Landscapes and Sunsets
10	Amazonian Canopy: the Roof of the World's Rainforest
11	Amazonian Tribes: a World of Difference
12	Birds and Butterflies of the Amazon
13	The Great Wonders of the Amazon
14	The Jaguar People
15	The Fresh Water Giants
16	The Call of the Shaman
17	Indigenous Families: Life in Harmony with Nature
18	Amazon in Peril
19	Giant Tarantulas and Centipedes

When I think of the vast South American continent, it is the mystery, natural beauty and indigenous culture of the Amazon rainforest that holds the most fascination for me. One is drawn to go deep into the heart of the Amazon basin to learn more.

Here in the Department of Loreto in the Upper Amazon, the vast jungle is home to wildlife and plants still waiting to be discovered. There are jaguars and monkeys of all sizes parrots and toucans boast their vibrant colours and pink river dolphins play while a group of children feed those pieces of fish bait. These children and their families are the river people, and these riverbanks are their home.

This is not a Hollywood style romantic environment. It's a place where if you take a wrong turn, Mother Nature can kill you; there is no room for arrogance and competition amongst humans. It's a strong and recurrent theme I witnessed throughout the rainforest: indigenous families working together for survival.

Upriver, canoe builders are busy constructing a new fishing vessel. They follow the trade of their forefathers—the best builders of handmade boats. Dug out canoes are hand-made from a single large tree trunk.

While I observe the jungle's wildlife and the playful pink dolphins, I cannot help but notice a unique feature in the lives of the indigenous river people, a genuine simplicity that is beautiful.

Although some indigenous people live in cities like we do, others still live much as their ancestors did thousands of years ago. The villagers organize their daily lives differently than we do in our western cultures. Their food, medicine, shelter and clothing come primarily from the forest.

Most of the children of the river don't go to school. Instead, indigenous children are taught how to survive in the forest and alongside the rising and receding waters of the Amazon River. They learn about their aquatic environment from their parents and the elders of their village. They are taught which plants are useful as medicine or food. These childhood experiences are the major factors that will influence their preferences and perceptions later in life. This "life school" will give them the ability to survive in a challenging environment.

The astonishing biodiversity of the Amazon River is the result of continual evolution, in which the people of the river have had to adapt themselves to the often hostile aquatic environment. The complex relationship between the indigenous people and their environment, between chance and necessity, has fashioned the living world in a multitude of forms. While biologists and anthropologists have already made great strides towards illuminating the extent and variety of the Amazonian web of life, our knowledge of certain indigenous groups is still very limited, in particular those who live alongside isolated tributaries or in areas difficult to access.

Nightfall in the Amazon rainforest is amazing because that is when living things get really loud. One species in this orchestra is the howler monkey. No night animal can imitate the call of the red howler monkey. It sounds nothing like any other monkey; it sounds like a combination of the wind blowing through the trees and large animal crashing through the brush. It makes one imagine a twister is about to hit, it rises and falls like the soundtrack of a thriller. For a visitor, deciphering the cacophony can be a challenge. This is why the Amazon rainforest is not for everyone, for even where it is not wild; it can be noisy, humid and steamy after the passing of a strong rainstorm.

One quickly learns that the jungle can be a brutal place and anyone with romantic ideas about living in the wilderness and surviving on what the forest has to offer should probably think twice. However, the excitement of being in the majestic beauty of the rainforest among the awesome birds, witnessing prehistoric fish that actually walk on their fins (evolution at work), making way for reptiles and insects crossing your path, listening the call of the howler monkey, and seeing pink river dolphins coming to the surface of the black water to breathe, makes all the discomforts worthwhile.

Decent trails through the jungle lead you to the next peaceful, friendly village where one sees kids playing soccer and basketball or swimming and diving in the river. Children who spot visitors excitedly show off their diving skills; villagers sit on their porches, or stroll along the clay walkways. Life sure seems sweet! It's almost like every day is a holiday!

Still, that does not mean that the rainforest is a theme park. There is a good chance one will come across a few unexpected things: a tarantula or a 6-inch flying cockroach, or an intense rainstorm.

Yes, being in the rainforest is an overwhelming experience. The vastness of the forest, the views of the rivers, the spectacular sunsets and sunrises, the smells, the sounds, the quality of the air, and the absence of anything modern or technologically advance fills one with awe. There are plants growing on trees that grow on even larger trees with beautiful flowers and impressive root structures. These are lakes so still they looked like mirrors. One can spend hours just taking in the sheer beauty of that overflowing, mysterious, dark, yet peaceful river.

While in the Amazon, a visitor can live side by side with the indigenous people. One can see them desperately trying to hang on to their traditional ways while adjusting to the new demands of the outside world. One can capture with photography the timeless aspects of their lives: singing, taking part in ceremonies, and bathing in the river.

It is the children though who seem to be most inextricably connected with the Amazon River. One day today's children will grow and have children of their own, as well as shouldering the burden of adult concerns. Yet, their connection to the rivers and tributaries will still endure, and it is this connection that they will pass on to their children.

What do the children of the river have to tell us today from their remote villages, in the center of the "lungs of the world," a vast rainforest that breathes for all of us? This is a story that needs to be told, of how these children and all our children are connected, all breathing the same air, all passing on a shared heritage and fate.

The Amazon Exploration Series Constantine Issighos

CHILDREN OF THE RIVER

The Amazon non-indigenous settlers have a long history with living in floating settlements. These settlements are both home and work place for the adults and the children.

Children attend school classes in one room floats.

The people are fishermen, fruit sellers and occasional labourers.

Homes have thatched roofs, without running water, only wood-fuelled stoves and no electricity.

There are a number of small floating settlements strung along the riverbanks.

The children of the river live a basic life, learning to fish and manage a canoe from an early age.

The river is their basic food source, means of transportation and their aquatic playground.

An occasional botanical floating medical clinic will visit the settlers to provide basic health care, courtesy of humanitarian groups and the local government.

Quite often, one can observe families going about their business in their floating rafts. Their floating rafts are trawling an underwater cage filed with live trout, river-turtles and other fish.

Once they arrive in the market, the children turn into "town-criers" as they try to outshout one another in their effort to sale their family's goods.